HOW A KING PLAYS
64 CHESS TIPS FROM A KID CHAMPION

HOW A KING PLAYS

64 CHESS TIPS
FROM A KID CHAMPION

Oliver Boydell

RANDOM HOUSE   NEW YORK

Text copyright © 2021 by Oliver Boydell
Cover photograph copyright © 2021 by Jonathan Barkat

Visit us on the Web! rhcbooks.com

Educators and librarians, for a variety of teaching tools, visit us at
RHTeachersLibrarians.com

Library of Congress Cataloging-in-Publication Data is available upon request.
ISBN 978-0-593-45126-7 (trade) — ISBN 978-0-593-51610-2 (ebook)

The text of this book is set in 11-point Dante MT.
Interior design by Larsson McSwain and April Ward

Printed in the United States of America
November 2021
10 9 8 7 6 5 4 3 2 1
First Edition

Random House Children's Books supports the
First Amendment and celebrates the right to read.

For My Amazing Mama

CONTENTS

A FEW WORDS FROM OLIVER

I am an eleven-year-old New York City kid with a passion for chess. I started playing this fantastic game at the age of five and immediately took a strong interest in it. Chess will always have a special place in my life. I can't imagine it ever *not* being an important part of my daily experience, of who I am now and who I will become.

It certainly explains this book. Not only do I love chess, but I also want to share the wonders of this incredible game with everyone. No matter one's age, language, culture, or background, there's value to be derived from playing chess.

My joy for teaching chess goes back to my days in kindergarten. I was thrilled to explain the game to curious classmates. I became especially excited when I could take a difficult idea and simplify it. I hoped to show that even a newcomer could appreciate the complex and intricate concepts of chess.

By the third grade, I was regularly getting opportunities to impart my excitement for chess to entire classrooms.

These classes largely consisted of beginners. So I had to be clear and understandable, without sacrificing the meaning of advanced concepts. Those invaluable sessions helped develop my presentation skills. As I got more practice and experience, I knew I could teach this marvelous game to a wider public. During the pandemic, I began to write—and soon finished—this heartfelt book.

There are many instructional chess books out there, but not so many that all chess players can benefit from, regardless of knowledge and experience. *How a King Plays* contains sixty-four essential chess tips, one for each square on the chessboard. I can't think of that number without immediately thinking of chess.

These tips are meant to guide the reader across the game's phases. The precepts mainly begin with the opening, proceed through the middlegame, and move into the endgame. But many of these tips are useful in all stages of the game. There are tactical thoughts, and then there are strategic ones.

With modifications, some of these principles can even influence everyday thinking. In carefully selecting the advice offered in my book, I looked for concepts that have worth both on and off the chessboard, gathered from my chess lessons, my own games, books I've read, and online chess videos. They can be absorbed easily and put to good use by anyone, from beginner to veteran player.

I hope you enjoy this book as much as I took pleasure in conceiving and writing it. I want to thank Bruce Pandolfini and Pradeep Pathak, and all my other coaches who have inspired me, and all those who have inspired them. Let's continue to inspire each other. It's said that a great journey begins with a single step. Here are sixty-four steps to move you ahead, along the right path.

PLAY FOR THE CENTER

A chessboard has 64 squares. The squares are all the same size—yet some are more valuable. The most valuable ones are in the center. Pay attention to the four squares in the middle of the board: d4, d5, e4, and e5. Chess players call that block of key squares the *center*.

From there, pieces have greater mobility. They can move to either side of the board quickly and easily. Imagine if key pieces are jammed on one side. It could take *all day* before they get to the other side. But if they're already in the center, a lot of time can be saved. It's one thing to put pieces in the middle and another to make sure they're safe there. Accordingly, don't just occupy the center. Try to guard it, too. That makes anything sitting there safer. It also makes it harder for your opponent to get active play.

So, to gain control of a position, play for the center right from move one.

DEVELOP ALL THE PIECES

Both sides begin with eight pieces and eight Pawns. The King, the Queen, two Rooks, two Bishops, and two Knights are the pieces. Chess players don't call Pawns pieces. All pieces start on their home rank, while all Pawns start on their second rank.

When you move a piece to a useful square, you develop it. You also develop a piece by moving a Pawn out of its way. Castling develops a Rook. By developing a piece, you energize it. The best way to gain control is to get all your pieces into action. Develop pieces so they can work as a team. Command them like an army. Position them to attack as a unit. Place them to support each other in defense. It's hard to do much with just one piece—even the Queen can do more when backed up. If you fall behind in development, you may never catch up. Your opponent's forces could beat you to the punch, and you might get checkmated, just like that.

So, for attack, defense, and control, develop your pieces as soon as you can.

CASTLE EARLY

The King is what the game is all about. It needs to stay safe. Get checkmated, and the game is over.

Many chess games begin by moving a center Pawn. The center might then open up, exposing your King. But you can get the King to safety, away from danger, by castling. Castling shifts the King to the side. By moving the King behind a wall of Pawns, it is tougher for your opponent to attack it.

Castling does something else—it activates the Rook. When castling, a Rook moves from the corner toward the center. Out of the corner, it's ready to be aggressive. Stay alert. Watch for chances to use the center productively, especially if there's an open file. You might be able to place a Rook on it. Then your Rook can attack the opponent's position.

So, unless there's a reason not to, castle early. It does two important things: it safeguards the King, and it develops a Rook. What a great start—attacking and defending at the same time!

PREVENT YOUR OPPONENT FROM CASTLING

Castling is almost always necessary in serious chess. It gets the King to safety, and it brings a Rook into action.

Chess is a two-way game: you try to build your position *and* prevent your opponent from doing the same. Playing for more space, you cramp your opponent. Arranging your Pawns nicely, you bust up your opponent's structure. Trying for double attacks, you answer threats against you.

There are two sides to every chess strategy. It's good to castle, and it's good to stop your opponent from castling. If a player can't castle, the King is confined to the center. Once stuck in the middle, it could become a target. Meanwhile, other friendly pieces might be unable to help. If the King is in the way, don't be surprised if friendly pieces become *un*friendly and stumble over each other.

So, as you do good things, prevent your opponent from doing the same good things. Castle early. Stop your opponent from castling at all.

AVOID MOVING CASTLED PAWNS

Castling mobilizes a Rook and gets your King to a safer place, with a wall of Pawns in front of it. If that wall is strong, enemy forces cannot get past.

Trouble can happen once you start moving those sheltering Pawns. Suddenly, weak squares pop up that can't be guarded well by Pawns or at all. Weaknesses, especially near your King, are attractive to your opponent. Opposing pieces try to occupy those weak squares.

Now and then, you need to move Pawns in front of your King—perhaps to drive away dangerous pieces, to keep pieces out of your position, or to create an escape square for the King. You might also need to make a capture, or there may be a clever reason for moving them. But never move them casually. If you do, you're stuck. Pawns are unable to move back to where they were.

So, for safety, think about which Pawns to move, or not move. Think how it affects your King.

DON'T OVERUSE THE QUEEN

The Queen is the most valued piece by far. Able to attack in all directions, it is a material-eating machine. A checkmating force. It can develop early in the opening. This tempts players to use it immediately.

The Queen is awesome, which is precisely what makes it vulnerable. If you bring it out early, it gets attacked. Too valuable to lose, it must usually flee those attacks. That wastes moves and time. Meanwhile, opponents build their position at your expense. Pretty soon, they're all set up, with their King safely castled. Imagine how hopeless your position could be. You may have developed only your Queen . . . and not usefully. Even the Queen needs helpers to be effective, which is why good players try to activate Knights and Bishops before the Queen. Then the Queen has support and can launch promising attacks and threats.

So, if the situation requires using the Queen, use it. Just make sure not to *over*use it.

DON'T GIVE POINTLESS CHECKS

The object of chess is checkmate. You should target the opposing King from the start, trying to get pieces out rapidly.

Let's say you develop a Bishop, giving check. You may not have considered the consequences. Suppose the check is blocked with a Pawn—you'll need to move the Bishop again, which squanders time and loses the initiative.

Checking is not automatically good, especially if it allows your opponent to take control. It's also foolish to check wildly with the Queen. Your opponent might answer such checks productively, and your Queen could get whacked around like a tennis ball. Checking for the sake of checking is silly—it gives opponents chances they don't deserve. If a check doesn't work now, save it for later, when it might be more useful, such as when you need a time-gaining move. Often, a nonchecking move is much better, a so-called *quiet move*.

So, avoid giving pointless checks. Don't wreck your game—check all checks before playing them.

REMOVE THE DEFENDER

If a piece is attacked and unguarded, it is "hanging." Hanging pieces can be captured for free.

Chess thinking is often about counting attackers and defenders. Suppose you're attacking an opposing piece with the same kind of piece. Is it guarded sufficiently? Yes, if the number of like defenders equals the number of attackers. Perhaps you could add attackers, if given the opportunity. Your opponent would then have to add defenders. Or maybe move the attacked piece away to threaten something else. The prey becomes the predator.

Instead of adding attackers, possibly the number of protectors could be reduced. Perhaps you can capture a defender, or drive one away with a threatening Pawn attack. Either way, by capture or threat, you might lessen a target's support. Then you can win it. This tactical motif is called *removing the defender, removing the guard,* or *undermining.*

So, when attackers cannot be increased, maybe defenders can be decreased. Less for them is more for you.

SEIZE OPEN FILES

The Rook is the second-most valuable major piece. Only the Queen is worth more. Knights and Bishops (minor pieces) develop easily. To develop Rooks, you need open files, which have no Pawns on them. A file is half open if it contains no friendly Pawns. Without Pawns in the way, a Rook has a clear line of attack into the opponent's camp.

You can open a file by advancing a Pawn in front of a Rook. The Rook's mobility increases as the Pawn advances. When your Pawn captures an enemy Pawn, that clears the file for the Rook already on it. In general, post Rooks on open files. You can strengthen the Rook's grip by placing a second Rook on the same file, doubling Rooks. Or back it up with your Queen, doubling major pieces. For further control, triple major pieces. It also helps to prevent enemy Rooks from opposing yours.

So, no matter how you do it—doubling, tripling, or preventing—seize open files!

"Chess is a war over the board."

—BOBBY FISCHER,
the only American World Chess Champion

GET FULLY SET UP

Bobby Fischer, the only American World Chess Champion, realized that "chess is a war over the board." War or chess, try to develop pieces to their best positions. But what is best early might not be best later. Opening, middlegame, or endgame, find the right place for each piece.

Much of the time, a Knight should develop to its Bishop-three square. After several moves, you may have an opportunity to improve its position, maybe to an ideal outpost square, protected by a friendly Pawn. It's even better if no enemy Pawn can attack it and drive it away. Bishops thrive on unblocked lines. Try to place them along clear diagonals. Rooks need open files. Post them on open and half-open files. Of course, there may not be such open lines yet, but prepare to open them with timely advances. Hold the Queen back at first. Bring it out when it makes sense. But be watchful—there could be problems. Finally, get castled. With your King in a safer place, you can really get going.

So, make sure you are set up and ready for business.

11

LOOK FOR ROOK LIFTS

Put your Rooks on open files—either open files or half-open ones. On a clear file, a Rook can move up to a more useful square. It might be able to get to the seventh rank, meaning the seventh rank from the player's point of view. In chess slang, a Rook on the seventh rank is a *pig*. Why? Because it can eat up a row of helpless Pawns. From the seventh rank, a Rook might threaten several Pawns. It also may serve another very useful purpose—it may cut off the enemy King from moving off the last rank.

But the seventh rank is not the only good spot for a Rook. Sometimes a Rook can jump up the file to a different post, maybe on the third, fourth, or fifth rank. You can then support the advanced Rook with a backup Rook, thereby doubling Rooks. This kind of movement is called a *Rook lift*. The lifted Rook might soon shift along the rank sideways to a better attacking position. It might even come all the way over from the Queenside to the Kingside, menacing the enemy King. It's an incredible resource.

So, give your attacks—and spirits—a big lift. Look for Rook lifts.

PIN AND WIN!

It's easier to checkmate with a stronger army. The stronger army is likely the larger one. You get a larger army by winning material. This is often about tactics.

Pins take place along a file, rank, or diagonal. They prevent something from moving off the line of attack. Why? Because a piece or Pawn on the same line would be exposed to danger, including capture. An absolute pin is one to the King. Whatever is pinned can't move off the line. Pins to other forces are relative. Moving out of the pin is possible. Absolute or relative, the pinned unit is vulnerable. Maybe you can capture it directly or put pressure on it, piling up on it. You attack it again and again. Eventually, it can't be defended—hopefully not well enough—and you win material. Pins can work even without gaining material. They keep the opponent on defense. But do not pin things automatically. Your opponent might have an unexpected trick.

So, check out potential pins before playing them. If they look good, my advice is to pin. They often win.

AVOID GETTING PINNED

Pins are weapons. They can win material, and they can prevent or discourage movement. In chess, we say the pin is mightier than the sword.

While it can be good to set up an annoying pin, there's another side to it: you should also avoid *getting* pinned. Once pinned, you must guard against losing material. Maybe you can cope with the pressure of being pinned, but your pieces become passive, and your position suffers.

Some pins are harmless: you can ignore them, or you can allow them, then drive away the pinning piece. Or you can put something in the way to break the pin. Other pins can be prevented by guarding a key square. It's best to do that with a Pawn, which might keep away an opponent's Bishop. But Pawn moves produce weaknesses and targets. Watch out if the Pawn move is near your King. The cure could be worse than the disease.

So, while you can usually survive being pinned, be careful. Scope out your opponent's pin ahead of time. Even better, try not to get pinned in the first place.

14

AVOID UNNECESSARY PAWN MOVES

Pawns do not capture the way they move—they move straight, but they capture diagonally.

Special rules apply only to Pawns, like *en passant*. Pawns are the only forces that can change into something else once they reach the last rank and promote. The values of the pieces are expressed in Pawns: a Bishop is worth three Pawns, a Rook five Pawns, and so on. Pawns cannot go backward. Push a Pawn and you are stuck with it. It can no longer guard the squares it used to guard. With no Pawn support, an entire sector is weaker. Pawns can fend off raiders. Without them, opponents invade the weakened squares. Those weak points are likely in your half of the board, possibly close to your King. You can sometimes correct a bad piece move by simply moving it back, but you cannot do that with a Pawn.

So, move a Pawn if it improves or strengthens your position. But do not move a Pawn without careful thinking. That Pawn can never go home again.

PLAY WITH A PLAN

Don't think only on your turn. Stay thoughtful while it's the other player's turn. Use your opponent's time wisely.

Decide future setups, what to do and how to do it. You almost need a plan to come up with a plan. And not just one plan—you will probably need several plans a game, right through each phase. Planning starts in the opening, even with the first move.

You can begin by asking yourself questions: How do you intend to develop your pieces? Which side is better for castling? Can the Rooks be activated? Are there promising Pawn advances? The answers to such questions should help you form a logical plan of attack.

Opening, middlegame, and endgame—always work with a plan. You may have to adjust plans. It depends on what your opponent does. But once you devise a plan, try to stay with it. Never change plans without good reason. Otherwise, nothing gets done.

So, stay on target. It's almost better to have a bad plan than no plan at all.

ASK HELPFUL QUESTIONS

It's the other player's turn. You're waiting for your opponent to move . . . but don't just wait.

Start asking helpful questions. What would I like to do if I could? This will assist you with planning. Are there weak points in my opponent's position? This will tell you where to attack. Do I have problems I should worry about? This will help you spot potential enemy threats.

You can prepare your defenses ahead of time. Are there tasks I must do? This reminds you to get your King to safety and to complete your development. Can I improve the placement of my pieces? This question guides you to certain strong squares. You can then maneuver a piece, maybe a Knight, to an outpost. Should I be simplifying or complicating? Trading or not trading? This comes down to basic strategy. Here is the point: be logical and relevant.

So, if you ask the right questions, you practically have the answers. Those answers suggest a path. Follow it to find your next moves.

"If you see a good move, look for a better one."

—EMANUEL LASKER,
the second official World Chess Champion

KNOW YOUR OPTIONS

Just like there might be more than one solution to a problem, there can be more than one strong move in a chess position.

Experienced players know not to play the first move that pops into their heads. Emanuel Lasker, the second official World Chess Champion, famously said: "If you see a good move, look for a better one." For any position, good players think of several moves before deciding the best one. These possible moves should respond to threats. They should also advance the player's own plans. Players make a mental list of these options, called *candidate moves*. There might be as many as four or five candidate moves. Players try to drop a few moves from the list, then analyze the choices that remain. That takes time.

So, search for options and compare candidate moves, but be careful not to run out of time. Do all that, and you might find the right move—the one that does the most and the best.

"The mistakes are there, waiting to be made."

—SAVIELLY TARTAKOWER,
Polish-French Grandmaster

CHOOSE REASONABLE PLANS

When you look at the board, everything is right in front of you. There is no hidden information. That does not mean decisions are easy—there's a lot going on. Savielly Tartakower, a witty Polish-French Grandmaster, warned: "The mistakes are there, waiting to be made."

Players often get sidetracked. After analysis, go with a reasonable plan. If ahead, trade down. If behind, avoid trades. If cramped, try to free yourself. If you have an overall advantage, develop an attack. If your King is endangered, get it to safety. Castle and keep out invaders. If you have a Pawn majority, mobilize it. If you have weaknesses, get rid of them. Trade bad for good. If your opponent is way ahead, it would be absurd to plunge into attack—you would be crushed by a larger army. Play a clever game instead—avoid trades, set up promising counterattacks, and play for the center.

So, plans should be logical, not wishful or imaginary. If you want plans to work, be objective. Base them on the facts . . . on the truth.

DON'T PLAY HOPE CHESS

Strong chess players do not rely on feelings, and they do not decide subjectively. They base moves on essential details, trying to be objective.

If a move looks good, players consider it. They look for future moves to back it up. If analysis proves the move to be strong, they play it. Players dismiss risky moves that cannot be solidly judged. Nor will they play bad moves on purpose. Unless terribly lost, they will not try to get away with something. They do not expect opponents to overlook things, to blunder. Good players do not play "hope chess." They know hope chess is bad chess. Gambling is not chess. A novice can refute bad play, even if by accident. In the opening, don't try to set up the "four-move checkmate." It brings the Queen out too early, it's easy to refute, and you may even lose your Queen.

So, play for the center. Castle early. Develop your pieces. Make sound moves based on logic. Don't fool around. Don't play hope chess.

DON'T RELY ON SHAKY DEFENSE

No enemy attacks should be ignored. Your opponent threatens mate with Queen and Bishop. You defend yourself, protecting the square on which mate is threatened. You do it with a Knight, developing to the edge.

Suppose you have overlooked something—your Knight can be captured immediately by a distant, previously unmoved Bishop. If you capture the Bishop, you might get checkmated. Therefore, you don't take back. You find another way to stop mate, but that loses a move, and the enemy Bishop escapes to safety. Your defense against mate was unreliable, and it cost you a minor piece.

Here's a different situation: you invade your opponent's territory with a piece that needs to be defended. Your invading piece is protected, and for now, you are okay. A few moves pass. Your advanced piece is still guarded, but the opponent suddenly removes your defense. It doesn't matter how you respond—something is lost.

So, be careful about questionable defenses. Constantly check them out. Move to move, everything can change. Do not count on what used to work.

DON'T BLOCK BISHOPS WITH PAWNS

The Bishop is a long-range weapon. It can strike from as far as seven squares away, corner to corner. The Bishop's distant power is why it's often preferred over a Knight. Knights need to be up close. But not every Bishop is great. There are good Bishops and bad ones. A Bishop is good when not blocked by Pawns. When blocked by its own Pawns, a Bishop is usually bad. A Bishop's problems are worse when the blocking Pawns are fixed in place.

Players often make the mistake of putting Pawns on squares the Bishop can defend, but that leaves squares of the other color unguarded. Whatever color the Bishop travels on, it's usually better to place Pawns on the other color. When so arranged, there are fewer weak squares, and the Bishop can move more freely. It's different when you have two Bishops, or a Bishop and a Knight—then squares of both colors can be guarded.

So, if you have a single Bishop, try not to put Pawns in the way. If you block up your Bishops, you shut down your game.

A KNIGHT ON THE RIM IS DIM

Pieces love to be centralized. From the middle, they can do more.

Sometimes it's smart to move a piece toward the edge. When this happens, it should be for a definite purpose. But be cautious about it. You don't want pieces getting stuck on the side. Knights confined to the outside can be terrible.

From the center, a Knight can attack eight squares. On the side, it can attack at most four squares. The corner is even worse—from any corner, Knights attack merely two squares. Not counting the King, the Knight is the only piece that cannot attack from far away. It just hobbles along with its L-shaped move. If your Knights are trapped on the edge, they may not get back in time, or at all. Paraphrasing Aron Nimzowitsch, the great strategist: "A Knight on the rim is dim—even grim." Dim or grim, a Knight's chances from the side are often slim.

So, unless there's a good reason, keep Knights away from the edge, where they might fall off the ledge.

KEEP YOUR FIANCHETTOED BISHOP

In many openings, you start by moving center Pawns. This allows your Bishops to come out directly.

There's another way to develop Bishops—on the side. So placed, a Bishop can aim at the center. This flank development is called a *fianchetto*. A fianchettoed Bishop can cut across the board, controlling squares on a key diagonal.

Such a placement is strategic. You can play a light-square game, with the Bishop aiming at e4 and d5. Or a dark-square game, with the Bishop targeting d4 and e5.

To fianchetto a Bishop, move a Knight-Pawn. This could somewhat weaken your structure, and your opponent may try to take advantage, possibly occupying the weakened squares. The squares are less weak if you keep your fianchettoed Bishop, so avoid trading that Bishop. Even if it wins a Pawn, it could be risky. Loss of the fianchettoed Bishop gives your opponent fresh points of attack. If that fianchetto is in front of your King, you could be in real trouble. Invaders can be pesky, and you might not be able to keep them out.

So, keep invaders out. Keep your fianchettoed Bishop.

PLAY FOR TWO BISHOPS

The Bishop has a positive side and a negative one.

With a clear diagonal, a Bishop can be an amazing attack weapon, able to strike from across the board. But Pawn barricades can be a problem, obstructing a Bishop's mobility. A Bishop can corral a Knight all by itself. However, a Knight cannot trap a Bishop without help. A Bishop can move and still control the same diagonal. A Knight can't do that. It winds up guarding different squares with each move.

A big snag for a Bishop is that it travels on just one color, while a Knight can guard squares of either color. This is where two Bishops are useful. In coordination, they can threaten every square on the board. If nothing is in the way, two Bishops can cause great damage. Think what they can do. They can work beautifully in the same direction, or crossing through the center from different directions. United Bishops are usually preferred to other combinations, such as a Knight and Bishop or two Knights.

So, play for the two Bishops, if you can. They can be an awesome force.

25

KEEP THE RIGHT MINOR PIECE

Strategic thinking starts early in a game—even before you get to the board.

As the opening develops, ask yourself helpful questions. What pieces will be important? How will the Pawn structure look? Which minor piece will be more at home? Some positions support a Bishop, and others a Knight. Some structures are better for a Bishop traveling on light squares, and others favor a Bishop on dark squares.

Accordingly, trade wisely. Try to wind up with the superior minor piece. If the position might become blocked up, keep at least one Knight. Perhaps you are heading to a Bishop endgame and have a Rook-Pawn. In that case, keep the right Bishop, the one that can guard the corner promotion square. If you're losing by a few Pawns, trade to get opposite-color Bishops. In that situation, one side's Bishop moves on light squares, while the other side's Bishop moves on dark squares. You might be able to draw by setting up a blockade on the squares your Bishop controls. The trick is to look ahead.

So, let strategy guide you. Make sure you have the right minor piece for what you need.

"Chess is the art of analysis."

—MIKHAIL BOTVINNIK,
the sixth World Chess Champion
and founder of the Soviet school of chess

MOBILIZE PAWN MAJORITIES

Mikhail Botvinnik, the sixth World Chess Champion and founder of the Soviet school of chess, stated: "Chess is the art of analysis." When analyzing a chess position, it might help to divide the board in half. In your mind, draw a vertical line down the middle. The half containing the two Kings at the start is always the Kingside. It stays the Kingside even if the Kings move to the other side. The half where the two Queens start remains the Queenside.

During a game, exchanges could shift Pawns to nearby files. The result is the creation of a Pawn majority. You have a Pawn majority when you have more Pawns on consecutive files than your opponent does. With a Pawn majority, attack by advancing it. Mobilizing the majority increases your space. It also gives you a chance to open lines usefully. If the opposing King is on that side, consider a full-scale Pawn storm. It could produce a winning attack.

Advancing a Pawn majority has the potential to create a passed Pawn. The defender will need to cope with it—to stop it from Queening. Serious concessions might be required.

So, first try to get a Pawn majority. Then create a passed Pawn. Advance it to the promotion square. Touchdown!

"The only good Rook is a working Rook!"

—SAMUEL RESHEVSKY,
eight-time U.S. Champion

PUT ROOKS ON THE SEVENTH RANK

The most common type of endgame contains Rooks. Fifty percent of all endgames have Rooks on the board.

Rooks are less important in the opening, when there's usually too much blocking the way. But as Pawns are traded, lines become unblocked, and Rooks can be more active. This is especially true in middlegames and endgames.

Rooks are long-range pieces. With no obstacles in the way, a Rook can attack up the entire board to the seventh rank. This is important for at least two reasons. It cuts off the opponent's King, possibly trapping it on the back rank. Also, a Rook on the seventh rank could attack several Pawns. Clearly, a Rook on the seventh is a powerful weapon.

So, put yourself in a strong position. Listen to Samuel Reshevsky, the great eight-time U.S. Champion: "The only good Rook is a working Rook!" Place your Rooks on the seventh rank and start munching.

CAPTURE THE RIGHT WAY

Sometimes you need to assess several ways to capture. When uncertain, take with the least valuable force. If mistaken, you probably have not made as big a mistake.

If a Pawn or a Knight could capture, generally take with the Pawn. If a Knight or a Rook, take with the Knight. At other times, it's better to capture with a piece—any piece, but not a Pawn. When capturing with a Pawn blocks up a key square or line, taking with a piece retains the option of moving it away. Maybe other pieces could replace it. Take with a Pawn, and it could become hard to unblock things. The Pawn might be stuck.

Suppose you could capture with a Bishop or a Queen. You must judge which piece to use. If it seems risky, take with the Bishop. If your Queen gives checkmate, obviously take with the Queen. There's nothing automatic here. How you capture should always be based on the situation.

So, whenever you have a choice, think it over. Capture the right way—whatever it is.

TAKE TOWARD THE CENTER

Two different Pawns can often capture on the same square. How do you choose which way to take? Should you capture toward the center? Or away from it? Analyze the situation before deciding.

Suppose you think it out carefully but remain uncertain which way to capture. I am going to say something that might sound strange: when you do not know what to do, you *do* know what to do. You simply fall back on principle. The principle urges us to capture toward the center.

This direction is usually better for several reasons. It's important to control the center, and more Pawns in the center can help you do that. Capturing toward the center can avoid giving your opponent a favorable Pawn majority. Taking toward the center might also open a Rook's line of attack. Rooks have greater flexibility when no Pawns block the way. They can then enter the game more easily. Occasionally, tactics require taking away from the center. Otherwise, rely on experience.

So, if unsure, go with principle. Take toward the center.

"An isolated Pawn spreads gloom all over the chessboard."

—SAVIELLY TARTAKOWER

AVOID PAWN WEAKNESSES

Three common Pawn weaknesses are isolated Pawns, doubled Pawns, and backward Pawns.

Pawns are isolated when no friendly Pawns occupy adjacent files to defend them. If attacked, pieces must protect, which wastes resources. The square in front of an isolated Pawn is often weak. No friendly Pawn can guard it. Tartakower advised: "An isolated Pawn spreads gloom all over the chessboard."

Pawns are doubled when they occupy the same file. Doubled Pawns occur by capture. Isolated doubled Pawns are extra bad. Neither Pawn can defend the other, and both can be attacked.

A backward Pawn is also a target. It can't move safely, even with a friendly Pawn next to it. Why? That nearby Pawn has advanced too far and can't support the backward Pawn's movement. Worse is when a backward Pawn is held back by a hostile Pawn. Major pieces might gang up on the backward Pawn from in front. Isolated, doubled, or backward, you don't need them. You do not want them.

So, unless there's a good reason, avoid Pawn weaknesses. Instead, force these problems on your opponent.

"Combinations have always been the most intriguing aspect of chess."

—ARON NIMZOWITSCH,
great chess strategist

SET UP YOUR TACTICS

There are five main double attacks in chess: the fork, the pin, the skewer, the discovered attack, and removing the defender. It's great when your opponent blunders into one of them. If that happens, take advantage!

But most good players are not going to ignore the obvious. They will defend themselves. Don't count on them missing direct threats, and don't expect winning moves to fall into your lap. Be more active and visualize ahead. Set up attacks beforehand, but don't automatically attack something just to attack it. If the attack can easily be answered, maybe hold back. It might become a stronger weapon later, by creating a second weapon. Combine the two, and you have a deadlier tactic. Nimzowitsch claimed, "Combinations have always been the most intriguing aspect of chess."

Or say you have a powerful pin. There may be no way to gain immediate advantage. If that's the case, don't necessarily capture the pinned piece. Instead, attack and pressure it until your opponent can no longer defend adequately.

So, play smart. Plan and set up your tactics ahead of time.

LOOK FAR ENOUGH AHEAD

Grandmasters can keep lengthy variations in their minds. Yet many positions are too complicated.

Even the best players don't easily see perfectly to the end, but it may not be necessary to look that far into the future. Visualizing a few moves ahead is often good enough. A half move is a move for one side. A full move is a move for both sides. Normally, good players try to look at least three half moves ahead. Players start by analyzing candidate moves. They try to determine their next move, which is a half move. Then they decide how the opponent might respond. That is a second half move. Players then try to figure out how to answer the opponent's imagined reply. All told, that is three half moves. Much of the time, strong players can and must look further than that. On the road to mastery, though, you are looking far enough ahead if you can visualize the next three half moves.

So, if you can see your move, their move, and your move again, you can play chess.

UNDERSTAND RELATIVE VALUES

Bishops and Knights are worth about three Pawns each. Rooks are worth about five Pawns. The Queen is about nine Pawns. The King does not have an exchange value. It can never be given up because, well, that's against the rules. Still, based on what it can do, a King is worth about four Pawns.

These values are relative and determined by the situation. Sometimes a Knight is more useful than a Queen. The Queen cannot give the same kind of forking check. Two Rooks are usually worth more than a Queen. Ten to nine. Still, watch out if the Rooks are undeveloped or poorly placed. An active Queen could be much stronger. It might mate or pick off one of the Rooks.

Combinations of pieces can affect value. A Knight and a Bishop supposedly equal a Rook and a Pawn, six to six. But a Knight and a Bishop can work together as a team. Together, they add up to about seven Pawns in value. Experienced players realize exchange values are not absolute. They are based on circumstances and are subject to change.

So, pay attention to relative values. It's not Einstein, but it is relativity.

TRADE WHEN AHEAD

Newcomers do not always understand the word "trade." They think it means to lose something. They wind up merely trying to capture lots of free things, even when there's nothing free to take. That's a losing strategy.

Throughout a chess game, you'll have opportunities to take *and* take back. You win material by taking more than you give up. You lose material by getting back less. Often, you get the same as you give up. That's a trade. In terms of material value, a trade is not automatically good or bad. The merit of a trade is based on another factor: whether it improves or worsens your position.

As a rule, you should trade when you have a material edge. Trading makes it easier to keep control, and it emphasizes your advantage. Four to three is good. Three to two is better. Two to one is even better. Another reason to trade when ahead is to eliminate potential counterattacks. If your opponent has nothing left, they are in trouble.

So, the logic is clear: when ahead, trade pieces!

35

DON'T TRADE PIECES WHEN BEHIND

It's bad chess to help opponents. This is certainly true for the strategy of trading. Players often trade at the wrong time or fail to trade at the right time. If ahead, trade pieces. When behind, don't trade pieces.

There are several reasons not to trade when behind. By trading, you increase your opponent's relative advantage. If you keep trading, you may have nothing left to fight back with. If behind, you don't want to simplify matters for your opponent, because that makes it easier for them to maintain control. By keeping pieces on the board, you keep the position complicated, giving your opponent a chance to make a mistake. You may even have prospects to save yourself. With stuff on the board, you can try counterattacks and tactical tricks. But take note: while trying not to trade pieces, it's different for Pawns, which can promote to a major or minor piece. Trading them might provide a surprising opportunity to draw, even if you end up behind by a minor piece. Your opponent may not have enough left to checkmate.

So, when behind, do the wise thing: trade Pawns, not pieces.

DON'T BE AFRAID TO TRADE QUEENS

Queen trades come up all the time. Trading Queens can be good or bad. It just depends.

Some players won't trade Queens at all, even if it wins a Pawn or messes up the opponent's position. They say things like "I need my Queen." I wonder what they need it for. Do they need it more than opponents need theirs? A Queen can move like a Rook or a Bishop. If players are good at moving the Queen, logically they should be good at moving Rooks and Bishops.

Many players overuse the Queen, and the rest of the forces suffer. The value of a trade hangs on circumstances. If trading improves your situation, do it. If not, don't do it. When you can win a Pawn with no problems, trade Queens. Eventually, an extra Pawn may become a new Queen. Besides, there's something more important than keeping your Queen: getting the opponent's King.

So, don't be afraid to trade Queens or anything else. Only trade if it's better than not trading.

"Sac, sac . . . mate!"

—BOBBY FISCHER

DON'T SACRIFICE FOOLISHLY

A sacrifice is a planned offer of material. It's almost always done for tactical reasons.

A gambit is usually a Pawn sacrifice in the opening. It's played to get an attack. If the attack is strong, the opponent will have to make concessions. Some gambits are gambits in name only, like the Queen's Gambit. The gambit is offered, but the player eventually gets the Pawn back.

Many so-called sacrifices are bogus. For example, you offer the Queen. Your opponent takes the Queen and gets checkmated. It's not a true sacrifice if you know you are going to win by force. Rather, it's a combination. You play a forcing move but have a planned move or series of moves in response. Perhaps you checkmate or win something. At the very least, you want to improve your position. It's okay to take intelligent chances and to offer carefully considered sacrifices. But do not give up the Queen, or anything else, without precise analysis. If the sacrifice makes sense, you may even end up with, as Bobby Fischer put it, "Sac, sac . . . mate!"

So, never sacrifice blindly or foolishly. It's better to make your opponent sacrifice their own pieces.

"The best way to refute a sacrifice is to accept it."

—WILHELM STEINITZ,
the first World Chess Champion

ACCEPT UNSOUND SACRIFICES

Many sacrifices are not true sacrifices.

A player offers what looks like a sacrifice, but it leads to something good, maybe checkmate or winning material. At the very least, the player's position is improved. Overall, nothing is really sacrificed, since the one who sacrifices comes out ahead on the deal.

If hit with one of these sham sacrifices, you probably have no choice. You take the sacrifice and try to minimize the damage. Sometimes, however, you do have a choice. You don't necessarily have to capture the offered sacrifice, especially if you're not being checked. When you really have a choice, think it over. If taking the sacrifice seems okay, take it. If it seems bad to take, don't do it.

Suppose after analyzing you can't decide what to do. Should you accept the sacrifice or decline it? Should you take or not? The practical answer is to take it—to accept it. That is usually the best way to punish unsound play. Otherwise, your opponent gets away with something.

So, follow the advice of Wilhelm Steinitz, the first World Chess Champion: "The best way to refute a sacrifice is to accept it."

39

DON'T BE AFRAID TO MOVE THE KING

If the center opens before castling, you could be in trouble. Maybe your King will have to move. If it does, you can no longer castle, even if your King goes back to its original square.

Sometimes an opponent unwisely sacrifices a minor piece to make your King move. Your opponent then realizes the error and hopes you don't take it. Maybe you will be afraid to lose the right to castle. But this is silly thinking. If you don't take the piece, you might be in a worse situation. A monster remains in the heart of your position. Why let Godzilla swallow you up? It's often safer to eliminate the enemy attacker right away, even if you're taking it with your King. True, you lose the castling privilege, but you may have a chance to "castle by hand." You simply move the Rook and King to their usual castling squares. Afterward, it looks as if you have castled. It takes a little longer, though you achieve the same result. Meanwhile, you have gained a piece, the one the opponent foolishly sacrificed and the one you wisely captured.

So, depending on the position, don't be afraid to move your King. You may lose the right to castle, but you do not have to lose the game. You might even win it.

ELIMINATE PROBLEMS

No matter how well you play, problems pop up. Pieces and Pawns are suddenly threatened. There can be Pawn weaknesses. The King may be endangered, now or in the future. Certain squares might need extra protection just to feel safer.

If you have time, try to get rid of pesky troubles and ward off potential ones. After analyzing your opponent's last move, answer all threats. Try to combine defense and counterattack with the same reply. If your King can be threatened, make sure you can cope with it. It's typical to give your King a way out. For example, you can avoid a back rank mate by making *luft*. *Luft* is a German word meaning space or air. In chess, it means to give the King an escape square. Do it by moving a Pawn, or if you're saddled with shaky Pawns, trade them for healthy enemy ones. In general, when you have weak forces and squares, guard and even overprotect them. Your position is sounder and stronger when you get rid of problems.

So, start eliminating problems. Give them to your opponent.

KEEP YOUR ROOKS ACTIVE

Rooks have power from a distance. In the endgame, they can attack the enemy King and Pawns from far away. Meanwhile, the King cannot attack back. The Rook is simply too distant, safe from counterattack.

If a Rook is far enough away, it has the "checking distance." Usually, a Rook doesn't do well in front of a moving Pawn. It does better behind it. But what if the Rook cannot get behind? Can it still be effective? When a Rook can't get behind, it might be useful from the side, along the ranks. It can then get the checking distance from the flank. Rooks should stay active. It may even be wise to sacrifice a weak Pawn or two in hopes of getting a dynamic Rook. This is especially true when pure defense drains resources. I'm not saying sacrifice Pawns mindlessly. Just don't give them away without a purpose!

So, play for active Rooks. Winning game plans seldom require passive Rooks.

"Pawns are the soul of chess."

—FRANÇOIS-ANDRÉ DANICAN PHILIDOR,
renowned eighteenth-century
chess player

ACCUMULATE SMALL ADVANTAGES

The player with the white pieces starts with a slight edge. But it's not a winning advantage. Whatever White does, Black can answer in a way that keeps it all even. The same is true if Black plays for a quick win. If both sides play the best moves, the game should theoretically end in a draw.

To play for a win, players need a strategy. Good players play positional chess, looking for advantages. The advantages can be tiny, apparently unimportant ones. The opponent winds up dismissing them or ignoring them.

Consider these examples: having more space, sounder Pawn structure, control of an open file, superior development, better minor pieces, or a safer King. Each of these advantages might be slight. None of them necessarily means much individually, but when accumulated, can add up to total control. To stop the mounting attack, your opponent may have to surrender something tangible, like a Pawn. Listen to François-André Danican Philidor, the renowned eighteenth-century chess player: "Pawns are the soul of chess." An extra Pawn can be a killer—it usually wins.

So, how do you get such an overall superiority? By steadily accumulating small advantages.

DON'T IGNORE ENEMY INVADERS

Your opponent's Knight crosses the frontier line, moving into your camp. But the Knight does not seem to threaten anything. In fact, after analyzing it, you begin to ignore it. You go on with your own game.

Several moves are played for both sides. You check the position after each of your opponent's next few replies. Those moves don't appear to threaten anything, and you forget about the Knight, the one that invaded earlier. Suddenly, that "harmless" horse becomes part of a crushing attack. Your position begins to crumble, and that's that. What can you learn from this? When opposing pieces invade your territory, certainly deal with immediate threats. Watch out, even if your opponent does not directly threaten anything. There may be hidden threats and future dangers. In just a few moves, those invading pieces could become monsters.

So, stay on top of things. If it's safe and you have the time, kick out those raiders right away. Don't let them turn your position into a landing zone.

44

AVOID PAWN GRABBING

Throughout a game, you'll need to know who has the advantage.

There are five main things to think about: material, time, space, Pawn structure, and King safety. The easiest to figure out is material. You can simply count pieces and Pawns. The stronger army usually wins. Naturally, you want to take stuff and get away with it. The most available targets are Pawns. Your opponent begins with eight of them, and some may become undefended. If you can win a Pawn without danger, you should take it. But taking it could be complicated. It may require a few moves of effort, and time could be lost. Move the Queen too much and you might expose your King to counterattack. If you go out of your way to pick off a risky Pawn, that's called *Pawn grabbing*. Taking a chancy Pawn has cost some of the greatest players famous games. Still, it's easy to be greedy.

So, don't take a suspicious Pawn without asking yourself this question: is it worth the trouble? Before grabbing anything doubtful, make sure you can get away with it.

BLOCKADE ENEMY PAWNS

Pawns can be dangerous, especially once they start moving.

Passed Pawns may rush toward promotion. Connected Pawns could take control of important territory. Your opponent might try to eliminate a weak Pawn by pushing it, hoping to trade it for a healthy Pawn of your own. You might be able to stop an advancing Pawn by blocking it. To prevent movement, occupy the square in front of the Pawn with a useful piece. This is called a *blockade*.

The best blockades cannot be broken. That is, no enemy Pawn can attack the blockading piece. Some pieces are good blockaders; others are not. It also depends on circumstances. The Queen can usually blockade okay, but you don't want it to lose mobility. Bishops are often good blockaders; so are Knights, particularly in the center. Rooks are terrible blockaders. They are easy to kick out by diagonal attack. You almost never want to place a Rook in a passive position. Instead, keep Rooks active. Let your King do the blockading. It can do the job and much more.

So, try to blockade enemy Pawns, but make sure you use the right blockading piece.

OCCUPY YOUR STRONGPOINTS

Mentally, the chessboard can be cut in half horizontally. The "frontier line" goes left to right. It separates your half of the board from your opponent's half.

When you cross that line, between the fourth and fifth ranks, you enter enemy territory. Do it carelessly and you will be driven back, which wastes time and can cost you the initiative. Queens, Rooks, and Bishops don't need to cross the frontier line to attack. They can do it from far away. But Knights need to be up close. A Knight is great when it can occupy a secure square across the frontier line, protected by a Pawn, when no enemy Pawn can attack it. Such a safe place is called an *outpost*. A Knight occupying an outpost can be an amazing weapon. It can't be easily chased away. When making plans or updating them, search the board for possible outposts. Transfer your Knights to them and overprotect those squares. Try to prevent the opponent from driving you away. Good strategy tells us to maneuver Knights to their best places.

So, occupy those strongpoints, and you're ready to launch winning attacks.

TURN PROBLEMS INTO SOLUTIONS

Sometimes you have a weak Pawn under attack, such as a doubled or isolated Pawn. Defending it may be too passive. It might tie down your pieces to pure defense. That could lead to a long and painful loss. Who wants to play on hopelessly for many moves?

There could be another way to go. Maybe you can sacrifice the weakness with purpose. Push the weak Pawn as a kind of battering ram. That is, sacrifice it. Possibly you could shatter your opponent's Pawn structure. Your opponent's King could suddenly become endangered. Throwing your weak Pawn into the fire might spin things around.

Suppose your castled King's position becomes exposed. Rather than leaving your King in place, where it could be checked, get it out of potential danger. Shift it to the corner, off the exposed file. Then use the open file for your own benefit, placing a Rook on it.

So, instead of being the defender, become the attacker. Make the problem the solution.

COMBINE DEFENSE WITH COUNTERATTACK

Your opponent builds up in a particular sector. Pawns are advancing against you. They are supported by a team of pieces. This onslaught can drive you back and cause real problems.

You could try to protect everything. It might work, but don't count on it. Even if you protect yourself perfectly, you're still being defensive. Offense is often the best defense. Of course, you must guard against direct threats. You don't want to be checkmated, nor do you want to lose material. Defend yourself, but add counterattack to the mix. Your opponent might get weighed down answering your threats. Suddenly, the attacks against you seem less serious—they may even stop completely. If opponents attack on the flank, hit back in the center. This usually works when their resources are being used elsewhere. Sometimes players attack on different wings, especially when Kings have castled on opposite sides, Kingside against Queenside. If you're in that situation, beat your opponent to the punch. Get your game going first, and do it all.

So, whenever you can, be versatile. Defend and attack at the same time.

DON'T OVEREXTEND YOURSELF

You want to win quickly, but do not try to win too fast.

Make sure you are set up properly. Otherwise, you might be unable to support your initiative. Attack too quickly, and you overextend yourself. For example, you might think about pushing Pawns forward to gain space and build an attack. Be certain you can defend those Pawns. Have pieces backing them up. Guard squares the Pawns would pass over. If you don't prepare, you might not be able to defend Pawns as they move ahead. After all, as they advance, they get closer to the opponent. The Pawns can then be attacked more easily. Advance too far and you bite off more territory than you can defend. Your pieces are likely to be out of position. They may not be able to get where they need to go in time. To defend your Pawn, you might have to neglect other duties. If the opponent can penetrate the over-stretched front lines, your King is in deep mud.

So, march ahead, but do it wisely. Plan all necessary safeguards beforehand. If you go too far too soon, you could overextend yourself.

MAKE YOUR OPPONENT OVEREXTEND

Players often overextend themselves, and that can lead to a quick loss.

Your opponent has a Pawn in the center. It's not defended. You develop a Knight to attack it. You're trying to lure the enemy Pawn forward into your territory. Your opponent could guard the Pawn but instead pushes it ahead. Apparently, your Knight must move, though not really, since you have a trap and don't have to move the Knight. Cleverly, you give a Queen check, which is also a double attack, menacing both the advanced Pawn and the enemy King. The rash Pawn will be captured next move.

At other times, you play a move that strengthens your position, yet this is not obvious. It looks like a blunder. The opponents are fooled, misled into lashing out unsoundly. They overextend their army. Their advanced force cannot be supported adequately, having rushed into the jaws of a clever snare.

So, encircle the invaders and destroy them. It is just like Hannibal against the Romans. You win . . . though without elephants.

DON'T AUTOMATICALLY MAKE A QUEEN

You have a passed Pawn. Naturally, you hope to promote it into a Queen. But there are times when making a new Queen is wrong.

Suppose you're winning easily. Don't make a new Queen if it stalemates your opponent. To avoid stalemate, perhaps delay promotion. Maybe promote to a Queen later. You may not even have to delay. You might be able to underpromote. Instead of making a new Queen, promote to a different piece right now. Making a Rook might avoid the stalemate. An extra Rook is still a huge advantage. At times, even a Knight could be better than a Queen. This is especially true when underpromoting to a Knight gives check. You might win the opponent's Queen with a fork. By promoting to a Knight while giving check, you freeze the action. That check could stop your opponent from mating you. I am reminded of a cliché: when it comes to promotion, less can be more.

So, do not automatically make a new Queen. Check first to be sure. In the magic of chess, it may be better to win the opponent's old Queen instead.

PASSED PAWNS MUST BE PUSHED

Time waits for no chess player. If you have an advantage, use it. Otherwise, it becomes worthless. Wait too long, and the advantage passes to the other side. Your opponent might have time to score with their own threats.

A passed Pawn is one whose advance no Pawn can stop. If you have a passed Pawn, your opponent must rely on pieces to stop it, and their resources are diverted to defense, which can slow down their attacks and plans. If you own a passed Pawn, consider its path to promotion. If it can't be stopped, get it going. Quickly move it up the board. But don't be rash. Make sure you can back up its advance. This could be done with a Rook, or sometimes a Queen. Either one protects best from behind, on the same file. The Queen is also great when centralized.

Position your forces to guard squares in front of the Pawn. The Pawn would then be supported on its march toward promotion.

So, don't let a passed Pawn just hang out. Use it as a weapon. If the road is safe, push it now!

ROOKS BELONG BEHIND PASSED PAWNS

Rooks need to be active. To be effective, they also like distance. A Rook prefers being far from its target. Then it can attack, without being attacked in return, maybe by the opposing King.

A Rook's connection to a passed Pawn can be critical. In the endgame, one of the Rook's functions is to support a passed Pawn's advance. Such a Pawn may have a chance to reach the last rank and promote. The Rook can help that advance by being on the same file, especially behind the Pawn. When placed behind, the Rook's mobility increases as the Pawn advances. Meanwhile, the defending Rook might try to block that advance, possibly positioned in front of the passed Pawn. That can be a real problem for the defending Rook. If it moves, the passed Pawn could then advance safely.

So, don't forget Rooks need space and distance to be strong. Offense or defense, they belong behind passed Pawns.

DECOY WITH THE OUTSIDE PASSED PAWN

Suppose you have an extra Pawn. That advantage is usually significant. With correct play, there's an excellent chance to promote. The Pawn could become a Queen.

But why wait to be up a Pawn? You might be able to threaten making a new Queen sooner, especially if you have a healthy Pawn majority. Try to advance the majority intelligently to produce a passed Pawn. A great weapon is an outside passed Pawn, which is usually off to the side, away from where the two Kings have castled. The Pawn can then serve as a decoy.

What is so good about that? Suppose only Kings and Pawns remain on the board. You can advance the decoy to lure away the enemy King. It would have to head over to stop the decoy, which could leave the other side of the board defenseless. Your King could then raid freely, meeting little resistance, attacking and winning the abandoned Pawns.

So, play to get an outside passed Pawn. Use it to decoy the opponent's King out of position. Then your own King can mop up.

PUSH THE RIGHT PAWNS

In the opening, advance Pawns that help development. Center Pawns are the best to move in the beginning. Rook-Pawns are the worst. They add little to development. But moving Rook-Pawns later could be good.

Suppose you are castled on the Kingside. Your King might need an escape square. Here, the smartest Pawn to move is usually the Rook-Pawn. Moving it tends to cause fewer weaknesses. On other occasions, it can be better to move one of the other Kingside Pawns. It depends on which escape squares the opponent can attack.

There are other potential problems. Make a bad Pawn move, and your King might get cut off by an invading Rook. Or you might be mobilizing a Pawn majority. According to Capablanca's Rule, start by moving the unopposed Pawn, which is called the *candidate passed Pawn*. It has no enemy Pawn in front of it. Moving other Pawns instead might make it hard to advance the candidate passed Pawn safely. Your Pawn majority then becomes useless.

So, think about your Pawn moves carefully. It's not always easy to make a good one. You have only eight Pawns at the start, and zillions of ways to push the wrong ones.

PLAY FOR PROTECTED PASSED PAWNS

As I've previously mentioned, passed Pawns can have great value. At the right time, they can advance toward promotion. To stop such advances, your opponent might have to make real concessions. But this isn't always the case.

Some passed Pawns are not strong at all. They might even be weak and attackable. That's where a *protected* passed Pawn comes in. This is a passed Pawn solidly protected by another friendly Pawn. Accordingly, the opponent can't use a piece to capture it without losing material.

In the endgame, with just Kings and Pawns on the board, protected passed Pawns are particularly valuable. The enemy King can't capture them, since the King isn't allowed to move into check. Nor can the enemy King unwisely move far away. If the King moves too far away, the protected passed Pawn could sprint toward promotion. Clearly, protected passed Pawns can be a huge advantage.

So, for real protection, aim to protect your passed Pawns with other Pawns. It's the best kind of Pawn insurance.

"The hardest game to win is a won game."

—EMANUEL LASKER

KEEP ENOUGH TO WIN

With a material advantage, checkmate can usually be forced sooner or later.

An extra Pawn is important. It could eventually be promoted into a Queen, or another piece. An extra Queen almost always wins. Newcomers sometimes make too many Queens. They delay giving checkmate. Instead, they gobble up everything in sight. There's no need to capture the opponent's entire army. Once you have control, use it to force checkmate. If you have an extra Queen, you don't need two extra Queens. Getting a bunch of Queens, while eating all the opposing Pawns before heading to checkmate, might seem appealing, but it's bad strategy. If the opponent has nothing else left, you might trip into an accidental stalemate. Once you get way ahead, don't fool around. I am reminded of Lasker's observation: "The hardest game to win is a won game." All your efforts should be focused on checkmating, and nothing else. Nor must you keep all your material, with checkmate in sight.

So, purposely give up some material if it helps you win sooner or if it makes your job easier. You don't need to keep everything—just enough to win.

"The King . . . becomes in the endgame a very important and aggressive piece."

—JOSÉ RAÚL CAPABLANCA,
one of the game's most revered and natural players

58

THE KING IS A STRONG PIECE

The King is the most essential piece. It's also the most threatened one.

The greatest risk to the King often happens early in the game. If you waste time, you will not develop fast enough, and your King could get trapped in the middle. With your King stuck on its starting square, you could lose very quickly. But that happens mainly in the opening, not so much in the endgame. It's different once a batch of pieces come off the board. The King can then move around with less risk. José Raúl Capablanca, one of the game's most revered and natural players, advised: "The King . . . becomes in the endgame a very important and aggressive piece." As the endgame begins, bring the King back to the center, where it can become an extra weapon.

Picture the advantage you might have: your King gets into the fight, while your opponent's King hides in a corner. It stays out of play, and your King can have a field day. Truth is, the King is a strong piece. It guards all the squares surrounding it.

So, in the endgame, take advantage of the King's strength. Be bold. Use your King actively.

KEEP OUT THE ENEMY KING

As the endgame begins, players start to activate their Kings. You should do what you can to limit the opposing King's participation.

One of the best weapons in this matchup is a Rook. It can guard an entire line of squares, even from far away. For example, you can place your Rook to cut off the opposing King. With such a barrier, the enemy King will be unable to cross the cutoff line.

Suppose your own King gets cut off that way. What should you do? You could try to oppose the opponent's Rook with one of your own. That could break the cutoff. With the barrier gone, your King could resume the fight. Now there's another tool at your disposal, a different weapon to limit the other side's King—your own King. Start moving it before your opponent's King can approach.

So, get your King to the right place faster. Then your King and Rook can work as a team. Your Rook puts up a fence while your King stands guard at the gate, holding off the barbarians. Together, they fight a good fight. They may even keep out the enemy King.

TAKE THE OPPOSITION

In endgames with just Kings and Pawns, each King tries to get the upper hand.

The stronger King can play offense, advancing on the other King, or play defense, stopping the other King from advancing. A King can get this superior position by "taking the opposition." This term concerns the relationship between the Kings. It's about the fight for key squares. It's a negative concept. Neither player wants to move. Instead, you want your opponent to move, to give ground. Usually, the Kings "stand in opposition" when separated by an odd number of squares along the same line. If you "have the opposition," you have the advantage. The other player must make concessions. Hopefully, you can then exploit them. Sometimes you can have the opposition and still get nowhere. If your opponent has the opposition, you might even be losing.

So, when it comes down to Kings and Pawns, activate your King promptly. Pay attention to the other King and play it right. You might be able to take control of the position once you take control of the opposition.

OPEN A SECOND FRONT

You might find a weak point in your opponent's camp. Direct attention at it.

Suppose you can't apply any further pressure right now. Maybe you can turn your sights on another target. It would be terrific to discover a second weak point in your opponent's position. If you can't find one, perhaps you can generate one. Either way, you would have a second target to pressure. Russian chess trainers, such as Mikhail Shereshevsky and Mark Dvoretsky, call this "the principle of two weaknesses." Whether you find a second weak point or create one, your opponent has two problems: resources must be used to safeguard both targets, and defenses might become stretched. Eventually, you could let loose an organized attack against both vulnerable points. With the ideal setup and proper timing, you have a great chance to break through.

So, if you can't immediately make headway, try to find a second target. Prepare your weapons, wait for a timely moment, then launch simultaneous attacks against both weaknesses. Neither defense might hold up. If you can't overtake one place, maybe you can bring down both.

MINIMIZE YOUR LOSSES

Your Bishop crosses the frontier line, and you let your guard down. The Bishop becomes surrounded, caught in a Noah's Ark Trap.

If three enemy Pawns snare your Bishop, you're going to lose the Bishop no matter what. Why lose it for nothing? Get something for it, perhaps a couple of Pawns. If you give up the Bishop but get two Pawns in exchange, you lose only a Pawn in value. You lose something, though not as much.

At another time, your Knight gets trapped behind enemy lines. If you can't get two Pawns for it, take a single Pawn. Make the opposing King capture the Knight. How might that help you? The opponent loses the right to castle. That's worth something.

In other cases, your Queen could be trapped. Don't give up lightly. Sell its life dearly. Maybe get a Rook and a Knight for it. Together, they are worth about eight Pawns. Once again, you lose only about a Pawn's worth of value.

So, chess is like life. Where you can, minimize your losses. You might lose material, but you don't have to lose the game.

REPEAT THE POSITION

Why are certain moves repeated now and then?

A player moves a piece. The opponent answers, moving a piece in turn. On the next turn, the player withdraws their first move, going back to where the piece used to be. The opponent then does the same, moving their piece back. The player then plays the same initial move, starting the whole process again.

What is this about? Several things could be happening. Perhaps the player wants a draw. If a position is repeated three times, a draw can be claimed. But there's another crafty thing going on here. If the opponent plays the same move again, it tells the player that the opponent is willing to draw. That's valuable information. It means, psychologically, the opponent is not ready for a tough fight. There's something else. The repetitions give a brash opponent a chance to make a mistake. To avoid a threefold repetition, which would draw, the opponent might play an inferior move. Because of that, the opponent's game could fall apart.

So, whether to learn something—or to encourage mistakes—repeating moves can be a sly way to play. Put it to good use . . . carefully.

"Nobody ever won a chess game by resigning."

—SAVIELLY TARTAKOWER

FIGHT TO THE END

When losing, it's easy to give up hope. But remember the wise words of Tartakower: "Nobody ever won a chess game by resigning." So, stay objective. Don't be afraid to recognize that you're losing. Then get ready to resist. Hide this awareness from your opponent by putting on a poker face. Now your mind is free to think.

Begin slowing things down. Your opponent will unconsciously move faster. They might blunder. They probably don't want to fight anymore. They want you to give up, but you're not going to.

Instead, wear them down. Start with counterthreats and double attacks. Even if you're having trouble finding ways to win, you still might be able to draw. Half a point is better than no point. Perhaps you can lure your opponent into stalemate. Maybe the same position will happen three times—you could claim a draw. There's also the fifty-move rule, which allows you to draw as well. If they're really distracted, your opponent could possibly lose.

So, even when it seems hopeless, play like a champion. Remember, as Irving Chernev, a popular chess writer, pointed out, "Every chess master was once a beginner." No one ever won by giving up. Fight to the very end.

"Every chess master was once a beginner."

—IRVING CHERNEV,
popular chess writer

GLOSSARY

Backward Pawn A Pawn open to attack by a major piece along a file

Blockade A technique to prevent movement by occupying a square in front of a Pawn with a piece

Candidate passed Pawn In a majority, the Pawn most able to promote, since no enemy Pawn occupies the same file

Capablanca's Rule When activating a Pawn majority, push the unopposed Pawn first

Checking distance The minimum distance from the enemy King a Rook needs to be effective

Combination A tactical series with at least two moves, often involving sacrifice

Cutoff A barrier created by a Queen or Rook

Decoy An outside passed Pawn, used to lure away the opposing King

Development Getting a piece into action

Discovered attack Moving a piece or Pawn to uncover an attack from behind

Double attack Attacking two enemy units on the same move

Doubled Pawns Two Pawns of the same color on the same file

En passant A rule allowing a special kind of Pawn capture

Fianchetto Developing a Bishop on the side, to its Knight-two square, aiming it at the center

File A vertical row on the chessboard

Fork Attacking two or more enemy units with one friendly unit

Frontier line The imaginary line dividing the board in half horizontally

Half-open file A file with Pawns of only one color

Hanging Attacked and unguarded

Initiative Control of play

Isolated Pawn A Pawn with no friendly Pawns to either side of it

Kingside Vertically, the half of the board containing the two Kings at the start

Luft A Pawn move creating an escape square for the King

Major piece A Queen or a Rook

Material Pieces and Pawns

Minor piece A Bishop or a Knight

Noah's Ark Trap A stratagem in the Ruy Lopez opening by which three black Pawns trap a white Bishop.

Open file A file with no Pawns on it

The opposition In the endgame, the relationship between the two Kings as they approach each other, determining the advantage

Outpost A strong, occupiable square across the frontier line

Outside passed Pawn With Kings castled on the same side, the passed Pawn on the most distant file, which could be used as a decoy

Passed Pawn A Pawn whose advance no enemy Pawn can stop

Pawn grabbing Taking a risky Pawn

Pawn majority In any sector of the board, having more Pawns than your opponent

Pig A Rook on the opponent's second rank

Pin A line attack preventing a piece or Pawn from moving off the line

Queenside Vertically, the half of the board containing the two Queens at the start

Quiet move A useful move that doesn't check or capture

Rank A horizontal row on the chessboard

Rook lift Transferring a Rook up a file, so that later it can shift across a rank

Skewer A line attack that forces an opposing piece to move out of the way, exposing a piece behind to capture

Strategy General plans and goals

Strongpoint A solid Pawn supported by another friendly Pawn

Tactics Specific attacks and combinations

Weak square A square that cannot be guarded by a Pawn

ACKNOWLEDGMENTS

I haven't done many of these, but I suspect it's never easy to thank all the people who have contributed to the successful completion of a project. Certainly, I extend my gratitude to the entire amazing team at Random House Children's Books. Their diligence and tireless efforts are deeply appreciated. Heartfelt thanks must go to my marvelous editors, Tom Russell and Brett Wright, my managing editor, Jake Eldred, and my copy editor, Alison Kolani, for their meticulous review of every word on every page. Their insight and advice enabled me to make critical decisions on style, inclusions, and the ordering of all sixty-four tips. A sincere thank-you to April Ward and Larsson McSwain for their creative eyes and art direction. Their imaginative take on layout was nothing short of spectacular. I am truly grateful to Barbara Marcus, president and publisher of Random House Children's Books, for reaching out and getting the ball rolling, and for meeting my mother on the corner of Hudson and Reade.

Last but not least is my family. They have supported my literary aspirations and my chess pursuits all along, every day. Thank you to my father, Paul, for his love and for being so encouraging and motivating, and to my brother, Sebastien, my comrade, for all we've shared together. He is incomparable. Nor can I ever thank enough my extraordinary grandmother, Bà Ngoại, whose own written works filled me with a passion to write from the first days I could read. Finally, I couldn't have started or finished any book without the devotion and brilliance of my beautiful mother, Tiffany. Everything I do is inspired by her.

ABOUT THE AUTHOR

Oliver Boydell was born in New York City to a Vietnamese mother and an English father. A National Chess Champion and a New York City Chess Champion, Oliver developed a passion for chess at the age of five. He started competing in chess tournaments during the same year and is a regular contender at New York City, New York State, and National Scholastic Chess Championships. Oliver endeavors to become a chess Grandmaster. His first book, *He's Got Moves: 25 Legendary Chess Games as Analyzed by a Smart Kid*, was released in late 2020 when he was ten years old. Oliver is the youngest published author of an instructional chess book in the world. He has been profiled in the *New York Times* and the *New York Post* and has appeared on *Good Morning America*, where he was featured in an epic chess match against George Stephanopoulos. Oliver loves sports, especially playing soccer and skiing double black diamond runs with his older brother, Sebastien. Visit him online at oliverboydell.com.